THE
OF LOVE

Bless

A little
book of
guidance

CHURCH
PUBLISHING
INCORPORATED

Unless otherwise noted, the Scripture quotations contained herein are from the New Revised Standard Version Bible, copyright © 1989 by the Division of Christian Education of the National Council of Churches of Christ in the U.S.A. Used by permission. All rights reserved.

Scripture quotations marked (NIV) are taken from the Holy Bible, New International Version®, NIV®. Copyright © 1973, 1978, 1984, 2011 by Biblica, Inc.™ Used by permission of Zondervan. All rights reserved worldwide. www.zondervan.com The "NIV" and "New International Version" are trademarks registered in the United States Patent and Trademark Office by Biblica, Inc.™

This book compiles text from the following sources:
Paul Fromberg, *The Art of Transformation: Things Churches Do That Change Everything* (New York: Church Publishing, 2017); Milton Brasher-Cunningham, *Keeping the Feast: Metaphors for the Meal* (Harrisburg, PA: Morehouse Publishing, 2012); Renée Miller, *Strength for the Journey: A Guide to Spiritual Practice* (Harrisburg, PA: Morehouse Publishing, 2011); Margaret Guenther, *At Home in the World: A Rule of Life for the Rest of Us* (New York: Seabury Books, 2002); Verna Dozier, *Confronted by God: The Essential Verna Dozier* (New York: Seabury Books, 2006); Winnie Varghese, *Church Meets World*, vol. 4, Church's Teachings for a Changing World (Harrisburg, PA: Morehouse Publishing, 2016).

Church Publishing
19 East 34th Street
New York, NY 10016
www.churchpublishing.org

Cover design by Jennifer Kopec, 2Pug Design
Typeset by Denise Hoff

A record of this book is available from the Library of Congress.

ISBN-13: 978-1-64065-176-0 (pbk.)
ISBN-13: 978-1-64065-177-7 (ebook)

Printed in the United States of America

Contents

Introduction

*I pray that you, being rooted and established in love,
may have power, together with all the Lord's holy
people, to grasp how wide and long and high and
deep is the love of Christ, and to know this love that
surpasses knowledge—that you may be filled to the
measure of all the fullness of God.*

—Ephesians 3:17–19, NIV

At the 79th General Convention of the Episcopal Church in July 2018, Presiding Bishop Michael B. Curry called the Church to practice *The Way of Love*. This is an invitation to all of us, young and old alike, to "grow more deeply with Jesus Christ at the center of our lives, so we can bear witness to his way of love in and for the world."

With this call, Bishop Curry named seven practices that can help us grow deeper in our relationship with God, Jesus, and our neighbors as we also learn how to live into our baptismal promises more fully. In today's world of busy schedules, hurried meals, and twenty-four-hour news cycles, it is now more imperative that we make and take the time to center ourselves and follow the way of Jesus. This might mean revisioning and reshaping the pattern and rhythm of our daily life—finding a slice of time to center our thoughts on Jesus. Within these pages you will find ideas to engage in the practice of bless as you walk on *The Way of Love: Practices for a Jesus-Centered Life.*

To be a Christian is to be a seeker. We seek love: to know God's love, to love, and to be loved by others. It also means learning to love ourselves as a child of God. We seek freedom from the many forces that pull us from living as God created us to be: sin, fear, oppression, and division. God desires us to be dignified, whole, and free. We also seek abundant life. This is a life that is overflowing with joy, peace, generosity, and delight. It is a life where there is enough for all because we share with abandon. We seek a life of meaning, giving back to God and living for others and not just for ourselves. Ultimately we seek Jesus. Jesus is the way of love and that has the power to change lives and change the world.

How are we called to practice the Way of Love? Bishop Curry has named seven practices to follow. Like a "Rule of Life" practiced by Christians for almost two thousand years, these are ways that help us live intentionally in our daily life, following our deepest values. These are not add-ons to our day, but ways to recognize God working in us and through us.

Jesus teaches us to come before God with humble hearts, boldly offering our thanksgivings and concerns to God or simply listening for God's voice in our lives and in the world. Whether in thought, word, or deed, individually or corporately, when we pray we invite and dwell in God's loving presence. Jesus often removed himself from the crowds to quiet himself and commune with God. He gave us examples of how to pray, including the Lord's Prayer. "Will you continue in the prayers?" "I will with God's help."

Practices are challenging and can be difficult to sustain. Even though we might practice "solo" (e.g., prayer), each practice belongs to the community as a whole in which you inhabit as a whole—your family, church, or group of friends. Join with some trustworthy companions with whom to grow into this way of life; sharing and accountability help keep us grounded and steady in our practices.

This series of seven Little Books of Guidance is designed for you to discover how following certain practices can help you follow Jesus more fully in your daily life. You may already keep a spiritual discipline of praying at meals or before bed, regularly reading from the Bible, or engaging in acts of kindness toward others. If so, build upon what we offer here; if not, we offer a way to begin. Select one of the practices that interests you or that is especially important for you at this time. Watch for signs in your daily life pointing you toward a particular practice. Listen for a call from God telling you how to move closer. Anywhere is a good place to start. This is your invitation to commit to the practices of **Turn—Learn—Pray—Worship—Bless—Go—Rest**. There is no rush, each day is a new beginning. Follow Bishop Curry's call to grow in faith "following the loving, liberating, life-giving way of Jesus. His way has the power to change each of our lives and to change this world."

1 ■ How Do We Bless?

We know that, right from the beginning, we are stuck with one another. We are meant to be together in families, households, or communities of some sort. As Genesis 2 has it, Adam was living a carefree bachelor's existence in the Garden of Eden. He wasn't complaining, but the LORD God decided that he needed companionship or maybe a challenge: "It is not good that the man should be alone; I will make him a helper to be his partner." So God created all the animals and invited Adam to name them.

None filled the bill, although some probably came closer than others—I would choose an intelligent, friendly dog over a raccoon or skunk any day—so then, in the version of the story that makes good feminists bristle, woman was created from Adam's rib. That is how it all began: all the pain and wonder, the complexity and joy of people living together. And the rest is history.

We human beings are impelled to cluster together and to try to stay together, not just to reproduce ourselves but to love and support one another, to be faithful and forgiving. I think about this at weddings, when a new family has been created, and I can't help wondering: *Do they have any idea what they are getting into? Maybe it's better that they don't know.* I think about our innate need for connection at funerals, too, when we mark a break in the chain that has held a family together. It makes me marvel at the enduring power of love that has kept often unlikely and unlovely people knit together for years, for decades. It is easy to forget the heroism of day-in, day-out living together. We need our helpers and our partners—in our marriages, in our traditional or not-so-traditional households, in our communities whatever form they might take.

Life in the workplace is also life under one roof. We bump up against one another, we irritate one another, and we support one another—sometimes all in the same day. It is surely no accident that the psychological principles of family systems have been applied so successfully to the dynamics of the workplace. If nothing else, they remind us that we are not isolated people performing our own tasks, but that, for good or ill, we are interconnected in very human ways like biological families. Or, for that matter, like Benedict's monks.

When I am able to see my colleagues in this light, not sentimentally like the families extolled in greeting cards but as complicated human beings who are both like me and unlike me, I am enriched. We live together under rules spoken but more usually unspoken. As in a biological family, we know each other's strengths and fallibilities. I know that one of my colleagues always wants that desirable corner piece of the cake at a staff birthday party. I know that another can always be counted on to pick up the slack if someone falls short. I know who always arrives barely on time or maybe even late, and who is on hand five minutes early. They know the same sort of thing about me. For many hours of the week we live under one roof together. There may be bumpy places, but I cannot imagine working any other way. I have to wonder what it would be like to sit alone all day in a tollbooth on a bridge or freeway. It must be lonely to be all alone under that little roof.

Meandering through the dictionary, a favorite activity for many during attacks of procrastination, can teach us about the complex and unsentimental nature of our care for the stranger: the words "host," "guest," "hostile," "hostage," "hospital," and "hospitality" all spring from the same Latin root *hostis,* meaning stranger or enemy. To extend hospitality means widening the circle temporarily, perhaps taking a risk. Our generosity may be rejected, and we certainly dare not hope for thanks or reimbursement. To offer hospitality is an obligation. There is nothing soft or mushy about it. It has nothing to do with artificial standards of behavior.

Yet all too often "hospitality" conjures up images from my youth at the movies: lavish dinner parties that are impeccably served, and receptions filled with elegantly dressed people sipping champagne at Merchant-Ivory house parties. Yet true hospitality goes beyond rules and regulations; sometimes it even demands that rules be broken or at least stretched. True hospitality demands attentiveness, not so much paying attention to the placement of the cutlery on the dinner table, but attentiveness and openness to the *other* who has entered our tent. This means putting ourselves aside, at least temporarily, and suspending judgment as we accept that other as neighbor and kin.

To receive invited guests at a meal planned for the occasion or to welcome an expected overnight visitor calls for us to put ourselves aside, at least temporarily, and to make a space for them, to enlarge our domestic circle. We offer this kind of hospitality willingly, at least most of the time. It is pleasurable to imagine what food might be appealing, to consider what new book or recent copy of *The New Yorker* we can leave in the guest room, to make sure that the bedside reading light has an adequate bulb, and to check that the guestroom closet is not jammed with our own out-of-season clothes. There are other occasions of hospitality, however, that are more demanding. These are the ones that I try to avoid, especially when I am feeling overextended and crotchety: the urgent phone call from someone I find unreasonably demanding, just when I am running out the door; the impromptu pastoral conversation on a day when I could use some sympathy myself; the unwanted interruption of work or study or solitude under almost all circumstances. Then, too, not all the visitors to our inner space come from outside. We do not often think of offering hospitality to those under our own roof, but a generous response to family interruptions is an act of true hospitality. Our patience can wear very thin, whether we are responding to the persistent queries and petitions of a toddler, hearing unwelcome advice from our parents, or answering absent-minded, repetitive questions from a (usually) cherished spouse or partner. Blessing both the stranger and those closest to us is our daily work.

The very term "work of God" suggests so many things: obligation, responsibility, and repetitiveness. A task can be accomplished quickly, and then it is done, but work is ongoing. Ideally we should love our work, or at the very least be convinced that it is worth doing. Work is not always interesting or immediately rewarding; sometimes it is downright drudgery. We tire, we wonder why and how we have committed ourselves, we may even despair, but we keep on working. Sometimes we work alone, and sometimes our work is shared with others. In the course of a lifetime, we may experience many kinds of work: manual labor and menial chores, work that challenges our minds and work that deadens them, work that is important to our own well-being and the well-being of others and work that seems embarrassingly trivial, but (we persuade ourselves) is nevertheless somehow worthy and must be accomplished.

For many of us it is alarming to think about our daily prayer as work. Do we really need to take on more of it? Surely prayer requires an altered state of consciousness or some special spiritual gifts that have eluded us ordinary folk. Prayer, if we go beyond those glib assurances that we are keeping someone "in our thoughts and prayers," is a tough subject. Too often we assume that it is the province of the specialist, the spiritually gifted, the officially recognized saint or the guru—the picture of Bernini's statue of St. Teresa in ecstasy comes to mind. How on earth can praying in the kitchen or on the bus or maybe lying awake at night come up to *that*?

Years ago Dr. Benjamin Spock's *Baby and Child Care* was *the* parenting bible, not quite handed down by God on stone tablets, but coming very, very close to divinely ordained pronouncements. It was a good book, and a comforting one. Right at the beginning, he offered strong words of reassurance to anxious new mothers and fathers: you know more than you think you do, even if you have never been left alone with a screaming seven-pound stranger before. I realize now that this was a profound spiritual truth, applicable to all sorts of life's challenges but especially to our life of prayer. As yearners and seekers, we all know more than we think we do. In our own way, we can figure out how to go about the work of God. In other words, we can figure out how to feel safe and free as we grow in comfort with the practice of prayer.

"Practice" is an important word here. It suggests that prayer is something that we do over and over, for the rest of our lives. Some words from Artur Rubenstein's autobiography came to me the other day when I was musing about this mysterious work. At the time of his writing he was the foremost pianist in the world and could fill a recital hall just by showing up. So I was surprised and a tad disappointed when he confessed that he disliked practice and that he sometimes cheated by excessive use of the pedal. If you are not a pianist, you should know that holding down the pedal through a passage of notes creates a quite pleasant blur of sounds. The expert is not fooled, but we ordinary folk don't know the difference.

It has taken me a while to realize that Rubenstein could as well have been talking about any kind of meaningful work, including the work of God. At first I wanted to excuse him: he was a renowned musician—why on earth did he need to keep practicing? Surely he was entitled to slack off a bit and coast on his reputation. Maybe he was getting bored with Chopin and could find nothing new in his music. Yet even as he cheated—primarily himself—he recognized the need for the musician's equivalent of a rule of life. His fingers might fly over the keyboard because of his innate giftedness; but that innate giftedness could come to fruition only because of his lifelong commitment to the hard work of practice.

Like the rest of us, he could coast for a while, but he knew that too much lazy use of that pleasantly blurring pedal had placed him on a slippery slope.

Even those of us who are not Rubensteins know that faithful practice is rarely an ecstatic experience. There are, of course, those times of breakthrough, when we are aware that we have reached a new place or that stubborn old obstacles have just melted away. But most of the time we just keep at it and, unlike my disappointed young man in the church basement, we know that it is quite unlikely that we will be magically transported to another realm.

Similarly, our practice of prayer must be independent of our emotional state. Naturally we want prayer to be exhilarating: I want it to make me feel good and to leave me with the assurance that I have logged on to God's website and gotten through immediately. Yet all of us experience those dry times when we don't feel like praying, when there are too many other things demanding our attention, when God seems distant, when we are not sure that we believe in God, or even that God exists. Having a regular time and place for prayer can be a great help here: we turn up regularly whether we feel like it or not. In other words, we keep our appointment with God with the same degree of conscientiousness that we bring to our appointments with our boss or our psychotherapist or our spiritual director or the plumber who comes to unclog the sink.

We can come to the Bible with a new understanding of what it says that will itself be a new response to that revelation: that God came into history to create a people who would change the world, who would make the world a place where every person knew that he or she was loved, was valued, had a contribution to make, and had just as much right to the riches of the world as every other person. That is what the church is all about, to bring into being that vision, that ideal community of love in which we all are equally valuable and in which we equally share. Every structure of life comes under the judgment of that vision: our politics, our economics, our education, our social structures. Even the church! Nothing is exempt from that challenge. Every member of the church who lives and works in any of those structures or any combination of those structures is called to carry the message that this structure will be redeemed to the glory of God.

True religion binds together and undergirds all the structures of society as the redeemed people of God infiltrate those structures, changing the world. We act as if religion were a compartment separate from those structures. I think the first Christians were all excited about the promise of making a difference, of changing the world. The ecclesiastical structures had not yet emerged, but they were not long in emerging. They were in place before the biblical record was all written down. The problem—now as then—is holding the structures under judgment. Not that ecclesiastical structures in themselves are evil, rather they are always under judgment. The structures are there, not for themselves, but in order that the people of God may be let loose into the world.

2 ▪ Who Do We Bless?

Before we can work for justice, we have to see people as beautiful, not merely deserving. Our deep longing for justice in the world is met as we make real relationships with others. When we retreat into social isolation, there is an increased suspicion of those who are different. Suspicion leads to prejudice. Prejudice leads to violence. Violence leads to death. Social engagement is a starting point for dismantling violence and insisting that life is more powerful than death. It is about witnessing God's action in the world and then witnessing to it. More than anything, it is about seeing uniqueness, individuality, and unfamiliarity in others as beautiful. Social engagement is empowered by our mutuality, by supporting each other and recognizing our interdependence. This is a powerfully counter-cultural position for most of us.

Social engagement is the first step that the church must take in dismantling violence—both large-scale violence and micro-aggression. Congregations express their own style of social engagement uniquely: some take up direct charitable acts, some work in political activism. Regardless of the particular work that we take up, from feeding the hungry to lobbying elected officials, the best social engagement is both working for change and being changed by the work.

It is the work of our salvation to seek justice and serve one another. The work of liturgy, study, prayer, and conversation in our congregations effects a transformation of our personal lives toward an ever-increasing recognition of the humanity of others and the sacredness of creation.

This work for most of us is personally painful. It challenges our assumptions, but more profoundly it pokes at our scars. We are asked to investigate those places in our lives where our compassion is limited by our hurt, and we work toward being the people God has made us to be, free from sin.

This might sound very idealistic to you, and if you disagree, it might sound judgmental. Ultimately, the work of liberation is idealistic and hopeful. It is also concrete and personal. It is tender and teary eyed. It is collegial and movement building. It is brave, and it can be humiliating, which is fitting, as it is a facing into the forces of isolation, contempt, and greed, the same forces the apostle Paul warned about. "For our struggle is not against enemies of blood and flesh, but against the rulers, against the authorities, against the cosmic powers of this present darkness, against the spiritual forces of evil in the heavenly places" (Ephesians 6:12).

According to William Stringfellow, an Episcopal theologian, we are confronted with forces of evil in society that are as certain and powerful as death to the individual. But in the resurrection of Jesus Christ, we have a new way. The way of Jesus is the way of liberation, and it must be the work of his church.

That work is often visibly taken up by scholars, political figures, and authors. But I want to acknowledge at the outset that those who do the work of justice in most of our communities are unknown. History may understand the movements to be led by one or two charismatic individuals, but the social pressure that created a platform for a leader is often built by regular people, people like you and me, showing up and working in their own ways for a more just society.

The Episcopal witness in the world is particular to a place and time. We engage the ordinary stuff of life in our worship and take the sacred into our hands. We approach the divine with our own simple language, and we trust that God has made us to bear light in this broken world. In these pages, we will explore just what those common practices and commitments have led us to say and do over time, and how they might inspire us to witness in the days to come.

In the twenty-first century, we Episcopalians have work to do. First, we have to understand sin as an active force in the world around us, one over which we have very limited if any power. From there, we can recognize our desperate need for God. The response of God to sin and death is resurrection and the utterly improbable reign of God's justice.

If we seek to see the beauty of God's reign, we can also live as though it is true today. We commit ourselves to this vision in our baptism, and we participate in a foretaste of the reign of God's love in the Eucharist. From there, we are compelled to take it to the world.

We have many voices in the Episcopal Church to carry us forward. The words of Episcopal theologian Kelly Brown Douglas may be the most compelling in this moment:

We must dare to live proleptically, that is, as if, god's promised future is already. The manner in which we conduct our living should be but a foretaste of god's time. This means that we must live as if every single human being, regardless of their language, their color, their country of origin, their income, their education, deserves food, clothing, shelter, care, because they do. We are to live as if the bigotry, fear, stereotypes, and hateful "isms" that separate us one from another are no more. We are to live as if compassion not condemnation, justice not judgment, and righteousness not self-righteousness are the watchwords of our humanity. We are to live as if the peace of god that is justice has come to earth. Even if these ways of acting are not the ways of our world, we must be daring enough to make them the way of our living.[1]

---

1. Kelly Brown Douglas, "How Is It That God Speaks?," January 21, 2014, www.feminismandreligion.com.

3 ▪ The Practice of Blessing

Caring

The Old English word for caring—*caru*—means sorrow, grief, or anxiety. Although this is a surprising description of the word, it holds within it an aspect that is critical to the spiritual practice of caring. When we commit to the practice of caring, we become aware and attentive to the sorrow, grief, or anxiety that rises in us when we see others struggling and in need. It is, as Harold Kushner says, "running the risk of feeling." When we truly risk feeling, we are no longer able to ignore, avoid, or deny the reality of people's needs. The spiritual practice of caring begins when we decide to risk feeling.

There are many ways to take on caring as a spiritual practice. The foundation of the practice lies in the attentiveness we give to the movement of deep feeling we experience. This sometimes requires intentional focus if we are so accustomed to caring in our work that we are not as aware of our feelings when they are triggered by a person or situation not connected with our ministries.

In order to develop this kind of focus and attention, we need to open ourselves to the needs of others on a regular basis. We can do this by committing ourselves to a ministry that has no connection whatever with what we do in our daily work. Or, we might align ourselves with a community project that cares for the underprivileged in the community. Or, we might push ourselves beyond our comfort zones to give care to a group of people that we find difficult to accept or love. Or, we might enter into a relationship with someone who experiences hardship on a daily basis. Or, we might even travel to care for those in a developing country. When we encounter what we don't understand, what we are fearful of, or what is unknown to us, and feel the sorrow and grief of compassion growing in us, we are ready for the practice of caring.

Such radical compassion causes three things to happen in our souls. First, we grow in gratitude. We become grateful for the lives and blessings that we have been given, but even more we become grateful for the recipients of our caring. Through them we begin to see the places in our souls that have lain empty for too long. We gain insight into how those empty places might be filled. Hope begins to trickle into us and our hearts begin to gladden.

Second, we are diverted from our own struggles. As we notice and respond to the grief and sorrow that creep up in our souls, when we relate with those in need, we find that we are no longer so absorbed in our own dramas and story lines. As we open ourselves to what is outside of and beyond us, we are less fascinated with the often trivial stresses that occupy our mind and souls.

Finally, the practice of caring helps us pull back the mantle on meaning. The purpose of human existence, the power of God, the strength of human community is revealed in ways that had before seemed obscure. The practice of caring takes us out of ourselves and into the heart of God through the hearts of others.

Hospitality

The way to understand hospitality practice is to back into it. We often think of hospitality as little more than entertaining guests—family, friends, and sometimes, strangers. We put food in the eating place, drink in the drinking place, as a way of sharing hearth and home with others. Sometimes we're blessed and filled by our guests, and sometimes we just wish they would go home. Offering hospitality can be both energizing and draining, depending on our moods, the personality of the guests, and the degree of perfection we try to achieve in what we offer. At its foundation, we know that hospitality is simply welcoming others into our space and sharing the simple things of food and conversation with them. Yet, we can still make hospitality into a work of heroism to rival any fabulous dinner put on by the Queen of England. At the end of it, we're worn out and want to be left alone for a while. If this experience of hospitality sounds familiar to us, we may be hesitant to grasp on to hospitality practice as the best way to knit our souls into the heart of God.

So, it's best to understand hospitality by backing into it. Take a few moments to remember when hospitality has been extended to you. When have you felt truly welcomed? When have you felt truly included? When have you been so blessed by someone's hospitality that your own heart overflowed with gratitude?

We understand hospitality best by reflecting on the most profound moments of hospitality that have been offered to us. Most likely, the acts of hospitality that stand out in our memories are those that were simple and genuine. They may not have any connection whatsoever with food or drink or shelter. They may be simply moments when another person unexpectedly gathered us up into their circle of friendship, or accepted us as we were, or loved us in spite of ourselves. They may be encounters with people outside our ethnicity or social standing. They may be nothing more than a flight attendant noticing that we needed another bag of peanuts.

Henri Nouwen spoke about "hospitality of heart." At its core, hospitality is an opening of the heart. It really has very little to do with having friends or strangers over for dinner. Indeed, we can invite the poor into our homes for a meal three nights a week, but if our hearts are not open, we have not offered hospitality. This is what makes many of us avoid hospitality as a practice. We hesitate to open our hearts to the degree required by hospitality. Providing a meal or shelter seems more manageable than opening our hearts.

Opening our hearts means we really have to gather others in. Their problems, their dreams, the injustices done to them, the hopes that lie hidden in their souls, the joys that have taken them to heaven's doors—all these become a part of our own hearts when we engage in hospitality as a spiritual practice. The challenge of this, of course, is that the contents of our own hearts merge with those of our guest. This means that what is in our hearts is no longer front and center. It's no longer all about me. It becomes, instead, all about us. That internal shift can be difficult to make. It is particularly difficult when the ones we open our hearts to are completely unlike us. They may be of a different background, have a different educational level, enjoy different foods, have a career that seems strange to us, wear clothes that are offensive to us, have tattoos or body piercings that unsettle us, or speak, think, act, or feel in ways that are completely other than all that we find comfortable. It's much easier to have our favorite friends over for dinner and call it hospitality than it is to open our hearts to those who are different. It's even harder to then be asked to let the contents of their hearts merge with our own. Yet, this is exactly the invitation that hospitality practice offers us. The paradox, of course, is that when we have the courage to fully open our hearts to those we love, to those who are strangers, and to those who are as different from us as a coyote is from a dove, we find that, in the name of the Triune God, they bless us and our lives are never the same again.

Like other spiritual practices, hospitality practice needs to be done regularly and consistently. We may need to set a schedule in order to be faithful to our commitment to this practice, because it is so easy to avoid. In order to get the full benefit of hospitality practice, it is also important to step out in places where we've never been, to meet people we've not known before, to experience arenas of life beyond our familiar terrain. In this, hospitality practice is not only about gathering others in, but going where others are in order to open our hearts to them there.

Gratitude

In the regular run of a day, we often find ourselves consumed by events and encounters. We try to attend to what is right before us at the same time that we're thinking of the next situation ahead. Gratitude may flit across the canvas of our souls from time to time when we experience some unexpected moment of grace, but it does not usually flow like a steady mountain stream all through the day.

When we think of gratitude we naturally think of being thankful that something good has happened, or that we have witnessed something outside our normal experience that has left us feeling some measure of awe, or that something difficult has taken a turn for the better. We are not as ready to feel grateful in the midst of hardship and struggle, or when those we love suffer injustice or indignity, or when our dreams are dashed, or when our hope or faith is tried or lost. That's when gratitude seems an unlikely companion. We figure we'll feel gratitude when there's something to be grateful for—when things change and are back to the way we believe they should be.

In fact, it is possible to experience gratitude as a steady mountain stream running through our days, but only if we approach it as something that applies to all of life no matter whether the situations that surround us swirl like a tornado or whisper like a gentle balmy breeze. Gratitude is not really dependent on having something positive to respond to, but a way of life waiting to be expressed. When we focus gratitude only on one part of life—what we perceive to be the grace of life—we miss the subtler grace that is always present in darkness, in struggle, in difficulty. Gratitude shines a light on the darkness, the struggle, the difficulty and in the pockets of brightness, we notice the grace that seemed before to be hidden from view. Though we had not expected it, we find our souls filling with gratitude for that grace.

There are few spiritual practices as enjoyable and fulfilling as gratitude practice for two simple reasons. First, it lets us re-live blessing and grace and in this we have the experience twice. Just consider all the moments and experiences where the presence of God has been felt, the times when grace has hovered like a bank of coastal fog. Those memories are stored in our hearts and etched on our souls. Gratitude is the way we access them again and again. Gratitude practice invites us into the past where we experience those moments anew. Gratitude practice invites us into the present where grace peeks out like a wildflower in winter. Gratitude practice invites us into the future where we are expectant in the promise of grace yet to be revealed.

Second, gratitude builds on itself, and in this we find that even when we thought something had no redeeming value, grace still peers out like a shy child waiting to be coaxed out from hiding. Sometimes it's difficult to find that shy child in the midst of situations that damage our hearts, or leave us in darkness, or fling our joy out the window, or challenge every bit of faith we have. We are so consumed with seeing ourselves through calamity that most of our energy is directed toward "crisis management." We console ourselves with the belief that God is with us, but finding the good and the grace-filled in the midst of it all can feel impossible. Gratitude practice helps us go back and look more deeply for the grace that seemed so distant, but it also helps us develop the skill for spotting grace even in the most dire circumstances.

When we begin gratitude practice, it is good to determine the strength of our gratitude muscles. We can start by writing down one hundred things for which we are grateful. At first, we'll find that we write very quickly. Our mind seems to pop with things that make us feel gratitude. Before we are halfway done, however, we'll find ourselves going a little more slowly. The further we go, the deeper we need to dig. Toward the end of the list, we'll be looking for the smallest, most stealthy graces—and they will be there. When we finally complete the list, we will feel both a spiritual weariness and a spiritual rejuvenation. This exercise will be a jump start for regular and consistent gratitude practice. As we progress in the practice, we begin to find that, rather than being grateful in hindsight, our souls are on the lookout for ways to see grace and be grateful for it.

4 ▪ Specificity and Solidarity

In his epistle to the Romans, Paul exhorts his readers: "I appeal to you therefore, brothers and sisters, by the mercies of God, to present your bodies as a living sacrifice, holy and acceptable to God, which is your spiritual worship" (Romans 12:1). The Greek word λατρεία (*latreia*) can mean both "worship" and "service," which is to say we live out our faith in the way we respond to both God and to one another.

To follow the Way of Love is to both worship God and to bless those around us: to share our faith and unselfishly give and serve. Like the disciples, we are called by Jesus to follow the Way of Love. With God's help, we can bless the lives of those around us by sharing our faith and unselfishly giving and serving. In blessing, we not only ask God to let us see the world through Christ's eyes, but also to see Christ in everyone around us. The Christ in us reaches out to and connects with the Christ in others. This is what it means to bless in Jesus's name—to share our time, talents, and treasure with gratitude and joy, both as individuals and collectively as congregations. We can change the world one blessing at a time.

In his poem, "Vacillation," W. B. Yeats wrote,

> While on the shop and street I gazed
> My body of a sudden blazed;
> And twenty minutes more or less
> It seemed, so great my happiness,
> That I was blessed and could bless.

Blessing requires specificity. The grand esoteric themes of theology have their place, but love takes root in those specific moments when we voluntarily and intentionally enter one another's pain. "God so loved the world" makes sense when love has a name and is lying in the manger. The Incarnation (big theological concept) comes alive in the specific person of Jesus, God with us in all our off-the-rack-ness, in all our struggles, in all our, well, lives.

In the specific person of Jesus, God says "Me, too" in a way that had not been said before. The stories in the gospels are full of specifics, Jesus making particular movements, though not spectacular ones, to offer compassion and healing. He stopped when the woman with the hemorrhage touched his coat. He asked Zacchaeus if he could come over to the house. He wrote in the sand to move the focus off the adulterous woman for at least a moment. He offered Peter breakfast.

How do we explain God with skin on? We don't—we can't. When we look at the specific brush strokes of Jesus's encounters with those around him, however, we begin to get the picture, to see what Love looks like. Love lives in the looks, the touch, the simple words of affirmation, the daily acts of recalling the promises we've made and keeping them. Sometimes it sings in a song that carries a memory in its melody. Sometimes it whispers in a word of encouragement or connection. Sometimes it travels silently in a touch or an act of hopeful sacrifice. However it comes, love—blessing—requires specificity.

Jesus's ministry was not scheduled. Most all of his significant encounters with people happened in the context of interruptions.

Matthew, Mark, and Luke all tell the story of two people who came separately to Jesus, though their stories become intertwined. Regardless of which gospel account you read, the chapter before and the one after are chocked full of relentless need. What Jesus mostly did was pay attention as life happened around him.

On one particular day, two people found him almost simultaneously. First, Jarius, identified as a leader in the synagogue, pushed through to talk to Jesus because his daughter was dying. Mark says, "He begged repeatedly." It doesn't appear he was making a power move or demanding, but he was a man of privilege, used to being able to push through the crowd and talk to whomever he needed to talk to to get things done. Jesus went with him. There is no recorded dialogue; Jesus just went. As they were walking, a woman in the crowd who was hemorrhaging dared only to reach out and touch Jesus. She didn't have the position or confidence to speak up, so she just tagged him and caught the hem of his cloak. Jesus stopped and asked who had touched him.

We can only imagine the tone of the disciples' response: "In the middle of this crowd, you want to know who touched you?" We might even hear sarcastic laughter. But Jesus didn't move, as I am sure was true of most of the people pressed in around him. He waited for an answer. Sheepishly, the woman revealed herself, and Jesus comforted and assured her. But the time she took used up what was left of the girl's life because by the time the scene had played out, Jarius' servants had come to say it was too late. But Jesus kept going to the house, leaned down, and took the girl's hand and said, "*Talitha koum*"—"Get up, little girl." She awoke and they had dinner.

Our schedules control not only when we do things, but also what we pay attention to as we go through our days. We can choose to have eyes and ears for only what matters to us, or we can choose to make ourselves available to be interrupted. We can choose to attend to our world. Jesus stopped because he said he felt power go out of him. He knew someone was trying to get his attention. His point is well taken: if we start stopping, it's going to cost us something. We even say we have to "pay" attention." We can't touch one another without consequence. Then again, we can't just walk on by each other without a price either.

Donna Schaper retells her friend's story about her sister growing up in a small Oregon town. She was talking about one of her son's friends, a boy who was on probation from school because he had been caught drunk. One more offense and he would be out. She was comparing his experience with something in her own past. As a girl in 1959, she was pulled over for driving with a beer in her hand in this small town. She was so upset when the policeman stopped her that she threw the beer can out the window, in full sight of the cop. He charged her with littering. We have to help each other along and cut each other some slack. We become aware that we are gifted and burdened, burdened and gifted. We are mixed-up people still who hope to live well and do good.

Fundamentally we think small and ordinary is the route to large and important. We are joyful about how the small carries the large and the ordinary carries the sacred. We spend most of our attention on incarnational thinking during the Christmas season. Many complain about how commercial Christmas has become. These laments miss the point of Christmas because Christmas is about commerce. It is about the ordinary carrying the holy. The carols all sing about a God from heaven to earth come down. Getting the Christ back in Christmas is not something we do in church, but something we can also do at the mall. Imagine that: holy behavior in public worlds, holy living in living rooms and kitchens, holy living in boardrooms and Congress. That is what the incarnation means. *Encarnacion.* Christ *con carne.* Christ in the meat. God is in the meat of things.

The prayer of confession in the Book of Common Prayer includes the particular phrase that asks forgiveness for "the things we have done and the things we have left undone."[2] In the call to do all we can to love one another and live together, often our omissions are those things that cause the cracks to appear, allowing us to drift apart without realizing what we have set in motion. Yes, we can and do inflict damage by what we do and say, still it seems what gets left undone soon becomes forgotten and paved over by life's other demands, burying necessary relationships like ancient cities under the dust and layers of modern life. Christine Lavin has an old song called "The Moment Slipped Away" in which she describes missed opportunities and things left

---

2. The Book of Common Prayer (New York: Church Hymnal Corp., 1979), 360.

undone—small, significant chances—leaving both her and the person unencountered lost in the wake of what might have been.[3] In gestures both small and large, what we leave undone opens a gap that gets filled with something other than love. Consistent, intentional, determined, tenacious love that leaves no stone unturned puts the solid back in solidarity.

It is hard to hear the word solidarity without thinking of Lech Walesa and the Solidarity Worker's Union in Poland, whose uprising in the summer of 1980 led to the overthrow of the Communist government there and contributed to the dissolution of Soviet control in Eastern Europe. They stood together and changed the world. In more recent days we have seen the same solidarity in various countries throughout North Africa and the Middle East. Walesa said, "The thing that lies at the foundation of positive change, the way I see it, is service to a fellow human being." He was awarded the Nobel Peace Prize in 1983.

Most of the noise in our world these days is divisive: we are labeled red or blue, black or white, right or left, right or wrong, us or them. War has become the descriptive metaphor of choice for the media. But listen—listen to the strain of hope underneath the cacophony of chaos. Listen to the daily fidelity that is marked by all those who get up every day and keep their promises. Hear the quotidian rhythm that is essential to the recipe for our connectedness. You can hear it in the word of a friend, in the bold

---

3. Christine Lavin, "The Moment Slipped Away," from the album *Beau Woes and Other Problems of Modern Life* (Rounder Records, 1987).

marching of an earnest throng, and the small gathering of people coming together to create a memory.

Jesus knelt among the gnarly olive trees in the Garden of Gethsemane to pray just before he was arrested for the last time, and he prayed, "Make them one." Not keep them safe or let them win or make them rich and powerful. Make them one. He knew what we all learn rather quickly as we grow up: the forces of life are fragmenting. We are pushed apart and pulled away from each other. We learn to blame and to betray. We learn to look out for Number One. We learn we can't take care of everyone, so we have to take care of ourselves. Not long before he prayed, Jesus sat with his disciples around the table and, as he served them bread, he said, "Every time you do this, remember me." What if we could hear those words as an invitation to communion and community in every meal, in every cup of coffee, in every beer at the pub: every time you eat and drink, look each other in the eye and remember me, remember the love that binds you and do whatever you have to do to forget the lies you have learned that tear you apart.

The point of life is not to be right, or safe, or famous, comfortable, or rich, or powerful. None of those is a sign of success or God's favor or significance, particularly when our power and wealth and safety require someone else to be poor and weak and scared. The point of life is to be together. To bless one another—all the one anothers—and to struggle against everything that leads us away from love. The point of life is to bless one another as we walk the Way of Love together.

5 ▪ Learning from Our Enemies

"What is the point," Jesus asks, "of loving only the people who love you?" This is one of his hard teachings, tucked away in the middle of the Sermon on the Mount. He makes it clear that it's not good enough to sort people into neat groups of acceptable and unacceptable, lovable and unlovable, keepers and disposables. And it's certainly not good enough to permit ourselves the luxury of hating our brothers and sisters, no matter how much we might feel that they deserve it. Love your enemies, he commands, and pray for those who persecute you.

We may try to persuade ourselves that Jesus was guilty of hyperbole here, maybe overdoing it to make a point or to set a high standard and play out little scenes in our imaginations, where we discuss the situation with him in a reasonable way: "Nice idea, Jesus, and I certainly understand what you're getting at. But you cannot honestly expect me to love X, Y, or Z!" Depending on the circumstances, it might be the neighbor who permits her dog— who is the size of a small pony and has a voice like the Hound of the Baskervilles—to bark lustily at four in the morning. It might be a political leader whose views about compassion and justice are radically different from ours. It might be the serial murderer whose face is on the tabloids at the supermarket or the parent accused of unspeakable child abuse or the drunken driver who killed a little old lady on her way to the bus stop. It might be a loved one who unthinkingly wounded us decades ago, and we remember the incident as if it were yesterday. It might be a friend who betrayed;

if we have lived long enough, we have all met Judas. So our nego-
tiations with Jesus go something like this: "Okay, I agree that
loving my enemies is a laudable goal, and I promise that I will
strive to achieve it. But in the meantime, isn't ninety percent good
enough? Or maybe even eighty-five?" Despite all our internal
equivocation, we know that his answer is a flat no.

Yet we are compelled to recognize the fact of enmity. To read
the Psalms on this topic is profoundly liberating, especially if we
contemplate those passages we never hear in church. Remember
that the Psalms are prayers offered *to* God rather than God's pronouncements on us, and as such they are powerful examples of
candor, shockingly blunt communication with the God to whom
all hearts are open, all desires known, and from whom no secrets
are hid. They make it clear that to be human is to have enemies,
to be human is to suffer from injustice and betrayal, to be human
is to yearn for vengeance. The bottom line: to be human means
that we are not as nice as we pretend to be. Psalm 58 is a particular
favorite on those days when I feel that the world is against me. It
is full of enemies who devise evil in their hearts; they are perverse,
liars from birth, and venomous as serpents. The psalmist's suggestions as to how God might punish them are even better:

> O God, break their teeth in their mouths;
>
> pull the fangs of the young lions, O LORD.
>
> Let them vanish like water that runs off;
>
> let them wither like trodden grass.

Let them be like the snail that melts away,

like a stillborn child that never sees the sun. . . .

The righteous will be glad when they see the
vengeance;

they will bathe their feet in the blood of
the wicked. (Psalm 58:6–10)

The psalm ends here, and we do not have God's reaction to this satisfying diatribe.

Who Are Our Enemies?

Often our enemies are faceless and far away: the people whom we have been taught to fear, the people who are very different from us, those who—we are persuaded—live only to do us harm. A common enemy can be a marvelously unifying force. So all Germans were demonized in World War I; even dachshunds fell out of favor as family pets, and Bach was suspect. We have record of the crude but powerful propaganda prevalent during World War II that uniformly portrayed all Japanese as physically repulsive and appallingly cruel. For decades we feared the godless Communists, but with the collapse of the Soviet Union they ceased to be the menace of the month. So now our all-purpose enemy is grouped together under the umbrella of "terrorist." It's a big umbrella, capable of sheltering the whole Muslim world. We appear to need enemies to understand and validate our own identity. The single-minded focus on an enemy assures us that we are righteous, that our reward will be to bathe our feet in the blood of the wicked. Ironically, we are outraged when we realize that our identified enemies have precisely the same intention toward us.

Then there are the enemies who truly wish us harm. Are we really expected to forgive them? If we took the gospel message seriously, we would see them as made in God's image, fallen but scarcely worthy of damnation.

It is easy and convenient to assign those whom we envy to the ranks of our enemies. Envy is a murderous sin, all too often confused with jealousy. If we are jealous, our affections are skewed, and we are lacking in generosity; we want the object of our love, whatever it is, all to ourselves. But if we are envious, we cannot bear the other's good fortune or talent. There can be no shared enjoyment or celebration: we want to kill the object of our envy. To identify these enemies requires that we look deep within ourselves and recognize our own capacity for sin. We need to ask ourselves, What can my brother or sister possess that arouses my envy to the extent that I do not want to possess it myself, but to destroy it? And, incidentally, to destroy them in the process?

Enemies might also be those toward whom we feel contempt and cold-heartedness. Hatred is so much easier than compassion, once we let ourselves slip into it. To view the derelict, the prisoner, or the addict as the enemy permits us to distance ourselves and avoid the complex work of blending mercy with justice. It also permits us to hold on to our fear, the fear of what the "enemy" might do to us. At the same time, it permits us to ignore the very real fear that comes with recognition of our kinship, that we are all—the most saintly and the most contemptible among us—made in God's image, fallen and yet valued. We would rather not claim my kinship with the killer or the drug dealer in the maximum-security prison, the deranged person begging by the subway station, or even the ordinary person with extraordinarily bad luck. It is much easier and more pleasant to identify them as the enemy and then, like the priest and the Levite, pass by on the other side.

Sometimes the enemy lives very close to home, under the same roof. The book of Genesis, that great family soap opera, provides plenty of stories of intimate enmity. Just look at Abraham and Sarah, our spiritual ancestors: there was enough going on in that household to run on television for several seasons. We have no idea how Sarah felt when Abraham uprooted the family. He said it was God's command, but it must have seemed crazy to a hard-working housewife already advanced in years. And on it goes: passing Sarah off as his sister, not once but twice, so that she almost ended up in Pharaoh's harem; bitter rivalry between Sarah and Hagar; the near-sacrifice of Isaac—no mother I know would stand for that! Think of the currents of enmity rippling through that household as Jacob cheats Esau of his birthright and then goes on to cheat his father-in-law. Out of jealousy, Joseph's brothers plan to kill him and then, in a fit of compassion, decide merely to sell him into slavery.

So why should we be surprised that all too often our enemies are very near us, that domestic violence—physical and emotional—is a daily fact of life? Or that wounds and grudges lie, unacknowledged and unforgiven, just beneath the surface in our very ordinary households? "Family" is such an inviting word, typically evoking warm feelings of safety and care, but ongoing proximity is not always easy. We grate on one another; we compete with one another; we hurt and betray one another. Siblings grow up convinced that their brother or sister is the favorite child. If a marriage lasts long enough, both partners will have accumulated a store of grievances, most but not all of them petty. It is often easier to forgive the faceless enemy half a continent away than it is to look with love at the imperfect people who share our homes and who have, deliberately or inadvertently, hurt us.

Sometimes the enemy is even closer to home. It is a cliché that we are our own worst enemies; clichés and hackneyed truisms exist because they are almost always true. In his letter to the Romans, Paul speaks for all of us when he exclaims that he does not understand his own actions when he does not do what he wants to do, but rather does the very thing he hates. In our failure to love ourselves as made in God's image, we can indeed become our own worst enemies.

Dobby, the servile house-elf in the Happy Potter stories, is so filled with self-imposed guilt, so quick with abject apologies for wrongs he has not committed, so assured of his own sinfulness that he is happy only when someone is beating him up. If no one obliges, he batters himself. Although he is a fictional character, something in him rings true: when we judge ourselves harshly, when we see ourselves as beyond redemption, we treat ourselves as the enemy. When we make choices that damage us, we become the enemy. Succumbing to harmful addictions, consistently failing to care for ourselves, misusing our God-given gifts, working ourselves to the point of exhaustion—all these behaviors make us our own enemy. In moments of self-awareness, we want to cry out with Paul: "Why am I doing the very thing I hate?" and then we continue to do it.

Forgiving as a Spiritual Discipline

"What is the point," Jesus says, "of loving only the folk who are easy to love—the people who are like you, who love you in return, who will only your good, who would never do you harm? That's no challenge at all!" When we pray the Lord's Prayer, whatever words we use—"forgive us our trespasses as we forgive those who trespass against us" or "forgive us our sins as we forgive those who sin against us"—it is very easy to pray the first petition and conveniently forget the second. Of course God will forgive our sins, assuming that we are at least moderately contrite. We are praying to a loving God, after all, a God who numbers the hairs on our heads and who cares what happens to us. But what about us? Are we up to it? Can we let go of our hurts and grievances and righteous anger so that our behavior can at least be a pale reflection of the prodigally forgiving love of God?

Whatever forgiveness is, it isn't cheap and it isn't easy. When it happens too soon, too painlessly, it is like a too-quick healing of a wound: there is healthy new skin on the surface, but deep down the hurt is still festering. A better image may be a great block of ice, melting slowly but inexorably. It cannot be hurried: there is no spiritual equivalent of the microwave. Sometimes it feels as if we are stuck, but if we let ourselves be open, the melting goes on.

We are each responsible for ourselves. Only we can forgive the sins or trespasses committed against us by another. Others can make suggestions, even voice disapproval, but we have to do the forgiving. Our relationship with our enemies is an intimate and ultimately lonely one. How we live into it is up to us. Jesus gives us a daunting example when he prays from the cross: "Father, forgive them, for they do not know what they are doing." Who are "they"? Most obviously, he is praying for his murderers—those who condemned and tortured him, and who are now killing him. He is praying for all those who hated and feared him and sought to destroy him, along with the soldiers who were "just following orders" and could not wait to divide up his clothing. What about Judas, the betrayer? He must be included—and Peter, who denied him out of fear after protesting his undying loyalty. Jesus's words from the cross deprive us of the luxury of the holdout, of hurt kept alive and our forgiveness withheld. We can no more forgive someone a little than we can be "a little bit" pregnant. Jesus did not look at the man with the hammer and say, "I forgive you, but I'm never going to forget this."

Most of our lives are lived on an embarrassingly petty scale—grudges nursed, hurts carefully tended so that they never heal. From the cross, Jesus rips our pettiness to shreds and shows us how enemies should be treated. His standard of forgiveness is radical, breathtaking, seemingly impossible. We may not feel up to the challenge, but we can try.

Who might see us as the enemy? It can be a painful exercise in self-examination to reflect on whom we might have hurt, diminished, or dismissed, intentionally or carelessly. And then to ponder: what will we do about it?

Who are my enemies? What can I learn from them? Justly or unjustly, those who wish us harm can teach us a great deal about ourselves. Are we being condescending when we think that we are gracious? Speaking harshly and hurtfully when we think we are helpfully direct? Coldhearted when we ignore the need of a brother or sister? Arrogant when we assume that our way—as an individual or as a citizen of a country—is the best and only way? If we pay attention and are willing to look at ourselves honestly, our enemies can teach us how to bless one another.

6 ▪ Social Engagement

God's promise is sure: wisdom is justified by her deeds. When we engage the world around us, we are transformed by the engagement. When we press through our fear to see the world as God sees it, we are transformed. When we dare to break the rules, to risk respectability, for the sake of God's Commonwealth of Peace, we are transformed.

There is that thing in our carefully constructed culture—even within our congregations—that doesn't like coloring outside the lines. Too often, we like to keep things nice and tidy. And there is something in us that objects to the yoke of Jesus when it takes us to places that we haven't been before—like a Eucharist with a mash-up of unlikely strangers, or a street protest, or a food pantry, or a foot care clinic for homeless men. We may object that the desire of God is too easy, the love of God is too free, and the mercy of God is too simple. The domination culture around us understands that getting things done has nothing to do with the character of God and everything to do with the simple application of force, violence, blame, and scapegoating. Sometimes it seems we believe the liberty of God must be stopped at all costs, because if God's offer of freedom is revealed to people, they will see that there is nothing to fear, that the yoke of Jesus will make all of us free.

Jesus offers an alternate reading of history—of my history, of yours—that promises us freedom from what we fear. Jesus says that everyone who is burdened and beaten down by the experiment of living may lay down that burden, lay down the lies with which they have made a life, lay down the fear that God's love is just too embracing, and take up the yoke which leads to the fullness of life, real freedom, and service to all people. God gives us freedom, which our Book of Common Prayer defines so beautifully in the prayer: "O God, who art the author of peace and lover of concord, in knowledge of whom standeth our eternal life, whose service is perfect freedom: Defend us, thy humble servants, in all assaults of our enemies; that we, surely trusting in thy defense, may not fear the power of any adversaries."[4] Jesus gives us a new story in which our peace is secured in service, and peace makes us free. It is in this freedom that we have the power to take up social engagement: our service in the world for Christ's sake.

This is how social engagement becomes an engine of transformation in congregational life: first comes our own desire to see justice in real ways in everyday life. Desire burns in us to the degree that we begin to notice ways that we might serve the cause of God's justice in the world. But that desire itself is not enough. We have to do real work in our lives, doing real service in the same Spirit that drove Jesus to pour out his life for the world. So, we go into the world as servants of God's mission. We experience the lives and needs of other people, perhaps strangers to us. When we have these experiences, we share them with other people. We may share our experiences with friends and family. Then we find ways

---

4. The Episcopal Church, "A Collect for Peace," The Book of Common Prayer (New York: Church Hymnal Corp., 1979), 54.

to share our experiences with others in our congregation, telling our stories as a part of God's story with us. When we share what we experience in our service to the world, it is an invitation to others to join us in the work. As a result, we begin to see people's lives, their actions, and attitudes, changing. New behaviors, new attitudes grow in us, informing our desire more and more. We continue to share our experiences and reflect on them with other people. Above all, we approach social engagement with humility, trusting that God is already at work making the world anew. This work is not confined to an elite cadre of the congregation; it is something that every member can engage. It is rooted and grounded in love.

Social engagement builds more resilient, sustainable congregations; and it works to free us from fear. While it addresses specific needs, like violence or homelessness or refugee resettlement, social engagement also nurtures relationships among groups and individuals who are strangers to each other. That is to say, it builds the Body of Christ. It takes people who have no reason to know one another and gives them the work of remaking what is broken in the world. This is why social engagement is an engine of transformation.

Before we can work for justice, we have to see people as beautiful, not merely deserving. Our deep longing for justice in the world is met as we make real relationships with others. When we retreat into social isolation, there is an increased suspicion of those who are different. Suspicion leads to prejudice. Prejudice leads to violence. Violence leads to death. Social engagement is a starting point for dismantling violence and insisting that life is more powerful than death. It is about witnessing God's action in the world and then witnessing to it. More than anything, it is about seeing uniqueness, individuality, and unfamiliarity in others as beautiful. Social engagement is empowered by our mutuality, by supporting each other and recognizing our interdependence. This is a powerfully counter-cultural position for most of us.

Social engagement is the first step that the church must take in dismantling violence—both large-scale violence and microaggression. Congregations express their own style of social engagement uniquely: some take up direct charitable acts, some work in political activism. Regardless of the particular work that we take up, from feeding the hungry to lobbying elected officials, the best social engagement is both working for change and being changed by the work.

When people give testimony to their work in God's mission in the world, it transforms the way that others in the congregation can imagine their social engagement. None of us can do this work alone; no one has the power to sustain themselves alone in working for social change. There will never be a perfect way of responding to God's call to serve the world's need. But when we testify to what we experience in the ambiguity of life, in trust and doubt, in personal relationships and loneliness, in the known and loved, and in strangers, the congregation gains a clearer picture of God's Commonwealth of peace. When we speak our personal experience to others, we tune the whole congregation to social engagement. Sharing our experience transforms us.

Blessing must be relational if it is going to work for our transformation. The work that congregations do is of a different quality than the work of a social service agency. Those agencies are essential to helping people and can effect change in ways that are profound and necessary. But congregations have a different concern. Our work of social engagement is personal; it is based on our desire to share ourselves with another person and be changed in the process. Social engagement in congregational life must avoid what Peter Buffett describes as "philanthropic colonialism," an attempt to solve other people's problems with little particular knowledge of or experience in those persons' particular context. Instead, we must strive to understand the ways in which we can, on the basis of our lived experience, enter the world in the Spirit of Jesus who longs to serve all people. The core of blessing is not how to figure out how to be more helpful in the world. It is learning how to be in the world in a way that is more receptive to being a part of it all.

When congregations take up the work of social engagement, it must begin by attending to the wisdom of those we are called to serve. We must honor the intelligence they have about their own needs, and how to meet those needs. Social engagement with people outside the congregation must reflect the way we want to experience all of our relationships within the congregation: with mutuality, respect, empathy, and love. Mercy, as opposed to judgment, must be the rule for social engagement in congregations. Turning away from judgment, while turning toward the virtues of mercy, love, respect, and dignity, changes the way we are of service in the world.

When congregation members take part in social engagement, their self-understanding and perspective on the world changes in deep and lasting ways. First, people experience transformation when they have personal interaction with those that they serve. Second, having an opportunity to reflect with others on their experiences of service is powerfully transformative. Without personal relationship and some kind of ongoing reflective process, people are less likely to experience long-term transformation. The influence of relationship and reflection changes people's sense of mutuality with others and makes them more generous and likely to take on social service. This also makes people less comfortable returning to old attitudes and practices. We find that there are many opportunities to reflect on our experiences. Sermon sharing—the work the people take on in completing the preachers' sermons—is one way. In sermon sharing, we always ask people to share their experiences, not their opinions. It is the lived experiences of each member that carry the wisdom of God, the presence of God that each of us encounters day-by-day in our lives. Opinions close down reflection from other people; opinions are like a line in the sand that you dare someone else to cross. Hearing others' experiences opens our imagination and wondering about our lives. This kind of work takes place in other places too: small groups, Godly Play classes, spiritual direction sessions, Bible study, and walks together at our parish retreat. The point is to keep the conversation going, not to imagine that there is an ending to it. God is speaking to each one of us, all the time; our job is to keep listening and share with others what we hear.

The call of Jesus Christ to share in God's mission lingers on our souls like a stain. Try as we might, we can't quite get rid of it. Social engagement is all about transformation, in the world and in our lives. Whether we recognize it or not, we are made a new people in Christ's resurrection. We become more familiar to ourselves as we follow his example, doing what he did, speaking what he said. Our desires begin to change; our priorities change. We become less concerned with fear and more concentrated on peace. And that stain just gets darker and darker, more and more and more permanent the more we take on the work of Christ in the world. When we act like Jesus, when we sneak into someone's life, we find out what it means to become the risen Christ in the world; the one who holds everything in his hands.

When we act like Jesus, we bless those around us.

TURN: Pause, listen, and choose to follow Jesus

THE WAY OF LOVE

*As Jesus was walking along, he saw Levi son of
  Alphaeus sitting at the tax booth, and he said to
  him, "Follow me." And he got up and followed him.
  – Mark 2:14*

*"Do you turn to Jesus Christ . . . ?"
  – Book of Common Prayer, 302*

Like the disciples, we are called by Jesus to follow the Way
of Love. With God's help, we can turn from the powers of
sin, hatred, fear, injustice, and oppression toward the
way of truth, love, hope, justice, and freedom. In turning,
we reorient our lives to Jesus Christ, falling in love again, again, and again.

For Reflection and Discernment

- What practices help you to turn again and again to Jesus and the Way of Love?

- How will (or do) you incorporate these practices into your rhythm of life?

- Who will be your companion as you turn toward Jesus?

LEARN: Reflect on Scripture each day, especially on Jesus's life and teachings.

*"Those who love me will keep my word, and my Father will love them,
  and we will come to them and make our home with them." – John 14:23*

*Grant us so to hear [the Holy Scriptures], read, mark, learn, and inwardly
  digest them. – Book of Common Prayer, 236*

By reading and reflecting on Scripture, especially the life and teachings of
Jesus, we draw near to God, and God's word dwells in us. When we open our
minds and hearts to Scripture, we learn to see God's story and God's activity
in everyday life.

For Reflection and Discernment

- What ways of reflecting on Scripture are most life-giving for you?

- When will you set aside time to read and reflect on Scripture in your day?

- With whom will you share in the commitment to read and reflect on Scripture?

PRAY: Dwell intentionally with God daily

He was praying in a certain place, and after he had finished,
  one of his disciples said to him, "Lord, teach us to pray,
  as John taught his disciples." – Luke 11:1

"Lord, hear our prayer." – Book of Common Prayer

Jesus teaches us to come before God with humble hearts, boldly offering our thanksgivings and concerns to God or simply listening for God's voice in our lives and in the world. Whether in thought, word, or deed, individually or corporately, when we pray we invite and dwell in God's loving presence.

For Reflection and Discernment

- What intentional prayer practices center you in God's presence, so you can hear, speak, or simply dwell with God?
- How will (or do) you incorporate intentional prayer into your daily life?
- With whom will you share in the commitment to pray?

WORSHIP: Gather in community weekly to thank, praise, and dwell with God

When he was at the table with them, he took bread, blessed and broke it,
  and gave it to them. Then their eyes were opened, and they recognized him.
  – Luke 24:30-31

Celebrant: Lift up your hearts. People: We lift them to the Lord.
  – Book of Common Prayer, 361

When we worship, we gather with others before God. We hear the Good News of Jesus, give thanks, confess, and offer the brokenness of the world to God. As we break bread, our eyes are opened to the presence of Christ. By the power of the Holy Spirit, we are made one body, the body of Christ sent forth to live the Way of Love.

For Discernment and Reflection

- What communal worship practices move you to encounter God and knit you into the body of Christ?
- How will (or do) you commit to regularly worship?
- With whom will you share the commitment to worship this week?

BLESS: Share faith and unselfishly give and serve

"Freely you have received; freely give." – Matthew 10:8

Celebrant: Will you proclaim by word and example the Good News of God in Christ?
People: We will, with God's help. – Book of Common Prayer, 305

Jesus called his disciples to give, forgive, teach, and heal in his name. We are empowered by the Spirit to bless everyone we meet, practicing generosity and compassion and proclaiming the Good News of God in Christ with hopeful words and selfless actions. We can share our stories of blessing and invite others to the Way of Love.

For Discernment and Reflection

- What are the ways the Spirit is calling you to bless others?
- How will (or does) blessing others through sharing your resources, faith, and story become part of your daily life?
- Who will join you in committing to the practice of blessing others

GO: Cross boundaries, listen deeply, and live like Jesus

Jesus said to them, "Peace be with you. As the Father has sent me,
so I send you." – John 20:21

Send them into the world in witness to your love.
– Book of Common Prayer, 306

As Jesus went to the highways and byways, he sends us beyond our circles and comfort to witness to the love, justice, and truth of God with our lips and with our lives. We go to listen with humility and to join God in healing a hurting world. We go to become Beloved Community, a people reconciled in love with God and one another.

For Discernment and Reflection

- To what new places or communities is the Spirit sending you to witness to the love, justice, and truth of God?
- How will you build into your life a commitment to cross boundaries, listen carefully, and take part in healing and reconciling what is broken in this world?
- With whom will you share in the commitment to go forth as a reconciler and healer?

REST: Receive the gift of God's grace, peace, and restoration

Peace I leave with you; my peace I give you. I do not give to you
as the world gives. Do not let your hearts be troubled
and do not be afraid. – John 14:27

Blessed are you, O Lord . . . giving rest to the weary,
renewing the strength of those who are spent.
– Book of Common Prayer, 113

From the beginning of creation, god has established the sacred pattern of going and returning, labor and rest. Especially today, God invites us to dedicate time for restoration and wholeness—within our bodies, minds, and souls, and within our communities and institutions. By resting, we place our trust in God; the primary actor who brings all things to their fullness.

For Discernment and Reflection

- What practices restore your body, mind and soul?
- How will you observe rest and renewal on a regular basis?
- With whom will you commit to create and maintain a regular practice of rest?

Little Books of Guidance

Finding answers to life's big questions!

Also in the series: